Credit Re~~~

Smart Guide to Improve Your Credit Score

NOAH FREEDOM

Table of Contents

Introduction

It might seem counterintuitive, but credit is an essential element to making your dreams come true and a critical factor in achieving financial independence. Whether you want to rent an apartment, buy a more comfortable home, get a new car or put money into your business idea, you can't do it unless you have access to credit.

That's precisely when you apply for a loan for something you need, that you face a problem you didn't even know existed: the credit score.

The credit score is the element that will determine if you can get credit and what interest rate you're going to pay for it.

A credit score is a simple number, just like your grades. This number shows how much creditworthy you are. Lenders look at that number to decide whether they're going to lend you money and how much they will charge you.

The higher the number, the greater the chances of getting a large amount of money at lower interest.

Credit scores are determined using a wide range of personal financial details.

Creditworthiness is associated with higher credit scores.

Financial institutions consider customers with better credit ratings to be less risky borrowers and offer them a wider range of credit products with lower interest rates.

In the sections ahead, I will reveal the secrets to repairing your credit, achieving a top-level credit score, and keeping it high and safe for a long time.

First, we'll see a short summary of credit history to understand how credit works today. In fact, the present situation is the collection of decisions, plans, and events that happened in the past. Figuring out where we are, it's crucial to know what our predecessors did and why.

After this short historical overview, we'll go through the essential knowledge required for this subject, put as simply as possible. Then you'll be ready to discover in every detail the journey of to build your excellent credit report.

Let's get started!

Chapter 1.

Essential History of Credit Score

Since the beginnings of the earliest agrarian empires, for more than 5,000 years, humans have used credit systems to buy and sell goods—that is, long before the invention of money. In this era, we also have a society divided into debtors and creditors who live in full cooperation.

The credit score is a weird bit of financial chemistry. Despite this, many Americans regard their credit scores—which claim to represent anything from one's credit history to one's debt attitude—as universal.

Of course, that isn't the case. Credit reporting as we know it today is less than two hundred years old, as it is part of the transition of America to capitalist modernity.

On the other hand, its history has been both painful and inspiring, allowing millions of people to achieve the American Dream through credit.

Moreover, it has instilled most Americans with a permanent financial identity: an indelible label representing past bad conduct and compelling future good behavior.

This past is more critical than ever at a time when credit reports are used to define a wide variety of decisions of life—from where they live or work to how much they will pay for services and insurances.

Credit reporting has become a profoundly personal activity for most of the debt's millenary history. For example, country storekeepers in 18th-century America earned loans by asking well-respected neighbors to put in a good word for their character to merchants and bankers.

And urban creditors scoured far-flung rural circles for gossip and hearsay about credit applicants.

Credit reporting started to modernize in the 1820s when the number of business transactions made with the previous methods turned out to be inefficient. Loans became riskier as a result of new bankruptcy rules.

As a consequence, a series of experiments in credit evaluation standardization were conducted. Though these tests were limited to commercial credit—loans to businesses—they would have far-reaching outcomes for consumer credit rating in the future.

The Mercantile Agency, established in 1841 by merchant Lewis Tappan, was the most significant of these experiments. After the Panic of 1837, Tappan set to work on systematizing rumors about the character and properties of debtors. Tappan's agency gathered information from correspondents across the country and distilled it into extensive ledgers in New York City.

These initial reports were influenced by their reporters' ethnic, class, and gender preconceptions. As a result, they were highly discriminatory.

The reports' subjectivity had two significant implications. Firstly, it acted as an early version of redlining, strengthening established social hierarchies. Second, early reports' jumble of rumors proved challenging to convert into actionable lessons.

What was one to make of reports like this one from Tappan's Mercantile Agency about Philadelphia merchant Charles Dull: "there is a good prejudice as being among the trade—usually enjoys a poor reputation as an individual, but is generally supposed to have money"?

Users of the Mercantile Agency and its competitor, the Bradstreet Company, started to demand a more straightforward assessment form.

The result was a brand-new phenomenon: a pseudo-scientific ruse that turned misinformation in borrowers' reports into financial 'facts' that could be implemented. Commercial credit ranking, which Bradstreet first introduced in 1857, took on a more stable form in 1864. In fact, during this year, the Mercantile Firm, renamed R. G. Dun and Company, created an alphanumeric system that would last until the twentieth century. (Dun & Bradstreet was founded when the two companies merged.)

Credit scoring was new in its own right, even though it was closely linked to contemporary innovations in population management, such as espionage and statistical analysis. According to scholar Josh Lauer, with its launch, commercial borrowers gained a 'financial identity,': an identifier to summarize one's financial history and affect his trustworthiness in case of a mistake due to destiny or discipline. About this development, one 19th-century commentator remarked that "the mercantile agency might well be termed a bureau for the promotion of honesty."

The three foundations of modern credit reporting were ready by the end of the Civil War:

- **private-sector mass surveillance** to make credit reports possible;
- **bureaucratic information-sharing** to make credit reports accessible;
- **rating system** to make credit reports actionable.

It would take about 50 years for all three of these elements to move from commercial to consumer credit evaluation.

In early America, consumer credit reporting, such as consumer debt, was useless. Consumption and production were closely interconnected, so a loan to a farmer for agricultural materials would be used to help him buy furniture and clothing as well.

However, by the last half of the nineteenth century, many Americans saw development and consumption as two different domains. Moreover, the labor movement's popularity meant that many people were working less while earning more.

Many retailers, such as newfangled department stores of America and the auto industry, extended great credit lines to get their hands on these workers' money. These credit lines helped many Americans gain access to the trappings of middle-class life.

The people in charge of evaluating consumer credit were not organized into a unique principal firm, as they were in commercial credit rating.

More often, they were employed as credit managers for retailers. Nonetheless, they used to adopt techniques pioneered by firms like Dun & Bradstreet.

In 1912, these credit managers formed a national association to improve methods for collecting, sharing, and classifying information on retail borrowers.

Many early agencies have had a short life, but firms like Atlanta's Retail Credit Company (RCC) had a lasting impact. Since its foundation in 1899, RCC acquired files on millions of Americans over the next 60 years.

This information included data on credit, capital, and character and information on individuals' social, political, and sexual lives. As a result, RCC was criticized, and the complaints against it reached a full peak in the 1960s when the company revealed plans to digitize its reports.

The reaction was fast and passionate. *"Almost inevitably,"* argued privacy advocate Alan Westin in a 1968 New York TIMES article, *"transferring information from a manual file onto a computer triggers a threat to civil liberties, to privacy, to a man's very humanity because access is so simple."*

As a consequence of the strong objections against the computerization of credit-reporting data, congressional investigations were carried out, and in 1970 the Fair Credit Reporting Act passed.

This federal law regulates the collection of consumers' credit information and access to their credit reports. It required bureaus to open their files to the public; delete data on race, disability, and sexuality; and **remove negative information after a specified period of time.**

Rather than blocking credit reporting, the FCRA opened its new golden era. The RCC, for example, came out of the Congress hearings seemingly defeated, but it did not disappear. Instead, in 1975, it was later renamed **Equifax** and kept going on its computerization path. Experian and **TransUnion** eventually joined it. They make up the so-called "Big Three" of consumer credit reporting.

Despite increased demand for their services, all three companies were troubled by issues that had plagued the industry for years: the difficulty of trying to interpret and evaluate their reports. To address this problem, they partnered with a tech firm to create a credit-scoring algorithm. Fair, Isaac and Company was the name of the company, which is now known as **FICO.**

Fair, Isaac, and Company were in a good position to handle this job. When the Big Three began their search for an industry-standard credit score, the firm, founded in 1956, was already selling credit-scoring algorithms for decades. The end product, released in 1989, was strikingly similar to the algorithm that is still in use today.

The FICO score, which was promptly adopted by the consumer credit industry, was the culmination of the process which started with the first credit-rating manual of the Bradstreet Company. With FICO, almost everyone in America would have a standardized financial identity. The financial identity had become a fact of life in modern America, no longer the exclusive domain of commercial borrowers.

Credit bureaus have significantly improved their methods to combine account data into borrower profiles. But they are not always accurate. In a 1989 study, Williams identified errors of this kind in credit reports over 10 percent of the time.

These errors sometimes are very harmful: for example, if the wrong information includes someone else's crimes, a person's credit rating will be negatively affected. Even if the erroneous accounts are in a good position, it seems that the applicant has more open credit lines than he or she actually does.[1]

---

[1] Hunt, Robert M. "Working paper no. 05-13 A century of consumer credit reporting in America", Federal Reserve Bank of Philadelphia, (dated June 2005)

1.1 What Can We Learn from This Overview of Credit History?

Credit scoring, as normal as it may appear now, is far from being universal. People in the past were right to be concerned about the accumulation of power in the hands of secret, private activist groups.

And now, these concerns are still alive. Credit monitoring, as in the past, can be used to support social hierarchies. Low credit scores, particularly among the more impoverished Americans, frequently turn into greater down payments and higher interest rates on purchases.

These terms put excessive pressure on household budgets and often lead to high rates of bankruptcy and default, which, consequently, lower credit scores even more.

However, not all of history's lessons are so negative. Credit reporting was crucial in allowing a wide variety of Americans to access financial resources, enabling them to purchase many life-changing products.

In the following chapters, we will see that you can use your credit report for your own benefit while it may seem like an obstacle.

In the past, credit was held in personal relationships that could be nurturing or predatory. Frequently they were predatory. FICO scores allow people to move easily between lenders.

Understanding the history of credit reporting shows that the purpose of the current credit score is the same as the written reports in Tappan's vast ledgers: to decide not only who can pay off their debts but who would choose to do so.

Credit reports allow lenders to make informed decisions about your creditworthiness. These decisions affect your life and determine your choices about housing, jobs, benefits, and utility costs.

We have also learned that credit reports are not perfect: mistakes may happen. These errors could negatively affect your scores and so restrict your access to loans.

According to a study by the Federal Trade Commission, around 25% of U.S. consumers discovered errors that could affect their credit scores in one of their credit reports.[2]

The same study stated that one in five consumers had an error that a credit bureau reviewed after the consumer disputed the mistake on at least one report.

---

[2] Federal Trade Commission. (2015, January 21). FTC Issues Follow-Up Study on Credit Report Accuracy [Press Release: FTC Issues Follow-Up Study on Credit Report Accuracy]. Retrieved from: https://www.ftc.gov/news-events/press-releases/2013/02/ftc-study-five-percent-consumers-had-errors-their-credit-reports

An error on your credit reports may result in lower credit scores and limit your ability to open a new credit account or get a loan.

In a specific chapter, we will see what actions you can take to ask the credit bureaus to remove incorrect records from your credit report.

Now that we have an essential historical background, we are ready to begin your journey with step #1.

Chapter 2.
Credit Knowledge

Now we can start with the blueprint to fix and boost your score. The journey is not complicated, but you shall know everything you'll be facing. Quite rightly, gurus who teach how to become financially independent emphasize that knowledge is power. To have the specific knowledge of each element related to credit is one of the fundamental pillars of wealth.

2.1 Types of Credit

Credit allows you to buy services or goods using borrowed money. The lending institution expects to get the payment back with additional money (called interest) after a certain amount of time.

There are three main types of credit:
- revolving credit
- installment
- open credit

Revolving Credit

A revolving line of credit is a kind of credit that comes with a capped limit and can be utilized until you reach the established limit. A **revolving line of credit** is usually offered by a financial institution. You pay the debt as you **would** any other. However, with a revolving line of credit, you can borrow up to your **credit limit** again without dealing with another loan approval procedure as soon as you refund the debt. If you exceed your limit, over-limit charges apply.

Installment

Installment loans are another kind of credit that involves a fixed payment schedule for a specified time. Installment credit is simply a loan for which you make fixed payments over a fixed period of time. Home mortgages, car loans, students loans, and personal loans are typical examples of installment loans.

Open Credit

According to research by the Federal Trade Commission, around 25% of U.S. consumers discovered errors that could affect their credit scores in one of their credit reports.

The same study stated that one in five consumers had an error that a credit bureau reviewed after the consumer disputed the mistake on at least one report.

An error on your credit reports may result in lower credit scores and limit your ability to open a new credit account or get a loan. In a specific chapter, we will see what actions you can take to ask the credit bureaus to remove incorrect records from your credit report.

Further on, we'll see that having a mix of the three credit types and managing them right is one of the winning strategies to lead your spending habits and improve your credit scores.

Before we get into the details of credit scoring, let's have a look at two critical subjects that are often confusing.

2.2 Credit Rating Agencies and Credit Bureaus

Credit Rating Agency and a Credit Bureau are easily confused, mainly because credit bureaus are often referred to as "credit reporting agencies."

Corporations and their debt issuances are classified by credit rating agencies such as Standard and Poor.

It helps investors to evaluate the riskiness of a business and its debt before making investment decisions. In other words, how likely is it that the company would default on its debt obligations?

Credit bureaus, like Equifax, are organizations that provide details about a person's creditworthiness. They give credit reports and credit scores to borrowers, such as banks, to help them decide how risky it is to lend money to a person. The stronger a person's credit profile is, the higher their credit score is.

A credit rating agency collects data on companies and nations, as well as the debt they issue, and assigns them a credit score to assess the debt's quality and risk.

Moody's, Standard & Poor's, and Fitch Ratings are the three major credit rating agencies.

Credit rating agencies are used by investors who choose to make capital investments in the hopes of making a profit.

A credit bureau is in charge of issuing credit reports and credit scores, which outline and rate an individual's creditworthiness and how risky it is for a borrower to extend credit to them.

TransUnion, Equifax, and Experian are the three major credit bureaus.

Credit bureaus are used by several businesses, including banks, landlords, and credit card firms.

Investors may use credit scores to learn more about debt commitments, fixed-income securities, and debt-based investment issuers. They're not the same as credit reports or credit scores. Credit ratings are collected and distributed by credit rating companies, of which Standard & Poor's, Moody's, and Fitch Ratings are the three major international players.

Credit rating agencies enable investors to evaluate the risk-reward potential of various investments and provide information on debt-issuing companies' financial stability. Insurance firms are also given credit scores to reflect their financial stability.

Credit ratings are provided in letters, like AAA or CCC, so that investors can quickly assess the risk of a debt instrument. The three leading organizations have different scores. You can divide these grades into two categories: investment grade and non-investment grade.

Many factors, including market-based, traditionally calculated details at the business level, might affect credit ratings. The assessments vary from company qualities to underlying investments, and they're all intended to assess the borrower's ability to repay its debt.

Credit rating agencies assess companies and their debt daily and change their scores based on their findings. When a company makes a significant choice, including incorporation, this is almost always the case. Rating agencies even rate countries' debt, which is referred to as sovereign debt.

Person borrowers' credit reports and ratings are collected mainly for lenders. Credit bureaus or credit reporting agencies are organizations that collect and disseminate information about customer creditworthiness.

The top three U.S. credit bureaus, Experian, Equifax, and TransUnion, regulate the market. The way information is shared a fascinating part of the credit bureau business model. Banks, retailers, landlords, and financing companies send consumer credit information for free to credit bureaus. The bureaus then sell the data back to the banks, financing companies, retailers, and landlords.

Credit bureaus collect and interpret customer credit assessments, which are used to determine credit scores. Credit scores are given a numerical value ranging from 300 to 850.

Your credit score has an impact on the loan amounts you can get approved for, the interest percentages you pay on those debts, and even your ability to rent a home or find work.

Upon request, each credit bureau will provide you with a free copy of your credit report once a year.

Both credit bureaus and credit rating agencies are heavily regulated, and their activities have been scrutinized more closely since the financial crisis of 2007-08.

Even though both credit bureaus and credit rating agencies offer financial info to the individuals, the types of information provided, the entities described by the data, and the people who handle the data are much different. The reason for accessing the information differs significantly between the two.

If an investor wants to invest $1,000 in the hopes of making a profit, he might consider acquiring a company's corporate bonds. Before making this investment, he might well check the company's credit information from S&P, Moody's, or Fitch to see how risky the investment is and how likely he will lose money. Access to this information is for personal gain.

On the other hand, individuals look at their credit reports only when they want to know their credit score. Only if a person applies for a loan or a credit card would a bank or credit card company access his credit information.

The bank, for example, will look at the loan applicant's credit record using details from the credit bureaus.

These details will allow the bank to determine whether or not the applicant has good credit and, if so, at what interest rate should be applied. The aim of obtaining access to this data is to control risk and avoid a potential loss.

2.3 Credit Score

A credit score is a number from 300 to 850 that indicates a person's creditworthiness. A borrower's credit score changes the way he or she appears to potential lenders.

A credit score is determined using information from your credit history, such as the number of accounts you have available, the total amount of debt you owe, and your repayment history, among other items.

Lenders use credit ratings to assess the likelihood of a borrower repaying a loan on time.

- A credit score influences a lender's decision to extend credit.

- Most financial institutions use the FICO scoring system.

- Repayment history, loan types, credit history length, and an individual's overall debt are all credit scoring factors.

- Credit usage, or the amount of usable credit that has been used, is one measure to determine a credit score.

- Closing a credit account not being used isn't necessarily a good idea because it can reduce a person's credit score.

- The Fair Isaac Corporation, also regarded as FICO, developed the credit score model, which financial institutions use.

- Although there are different credit-scoring systems, perhaps the most common is the FICO score. A person's credit score can be strengthened in various ways, including timely loan repayment and maintaining debt low.

2.4 Credit Score vs. Credit Report - The Key Differences

Since there are three, we can actually say "credit reports." In the United States, Experian, TransUnion, and Equifax have a trio of national credit unions competing to provide their customers with the complete details. These clients may include mortgage lenders, car rentals, insurers, collection agencies, tenants, future and present-day employers, as well as you.

Your credit report contains accurate details about your financial history of credit cards, loans, and charging cards compared to your credit score. There are four categories: identifying information, credit inquiries, credit accounts, and public records. Your credit reports would typically show you whether you commit any of your bills. It also provides the reader data on the amount, balance, and other details of accounts you have opened.

It can be very different for each study. That's why when evaluating your credit health, and it's necessary to look at all three. Your operation can find its way into all of your reports, depending on the lender's methodology. The details can, in other instances, be inaccurate or completely absent. An organization does not have to answer to any of the offices and all of them. And if the data is wrong or incomplete, it is not usually the responsibility of the office. In transmitting or transmitting data, the lender may have been mistaken.

You have the right to receive copies of your credit reports once every 12 months from all three offices. You could get them for free even better. The Big Three sponsors an AnnualCreditReport site that offers requests for your reports. The reports can be presented as part of a promotion or a paid affiliation by other sites. Some might try to trick you into believing you're on the official site.

You have the right once each year to have a free copy of each credit report, which can be obtained through the government-supporting Annual Credit Report site.

Many credit cards companies, particularly, do not care too much about what you report on. They don't want to digest all the information and evaluate how much credit risk you pose. Instead, they're paying for something else. While other markers, such as VantageScore, dominate the market, the Fair Isaac Corporation (FICO) usually uses the words "credit score" and "FIC Production" interchangeably.

Whichever organization you calculate, it summarizes the credit score, essentially a "credit report snapshot," according to Bethy Hardeman, former Product Marketing Manager at the Credit Karma, a credit advice site (much as your grade summarizes your performance in a course). You can score 300 or 850. You can score 850. The higher your ranking, the lower the chance. Five weighted groups are used to calculate:

- Payment history (35%)
- Length of credit history (15%)
- Amounts owed (30%)
- New credit (10%)
- Credit mix (10%)

Can you recall the three records by the credit office? Based on each of them, FICO calculates a ranking. Various lenders often use different scoring models — not just FICO — because there are usually multiple credit scores for individuals.

Unfortunately, as in your credit reports, you are not immediately entitled to collect your credit scores for free. Maybe you would pay for it. The Dodd-Frank Act allows you to see your loans from any borrower who used them to decide credit. It is also provided free of charge by several businesses through credit cards and other financial institutions. You can also receive a free score from advisory services like Credit Karma. But be careful: Some sites and services can give a "free" ranking and have costly subscription fees or other requirements you may not like.

The distinction between a credit report and a credit score is that the latter is a single numerical level.

At the same time, the second is a collection of data that gives a thorough examination of your financial statements.

They are different, but they are related as the result of the study. The lenders can both determine whether to grant you loans or not.

Your credit is valuable, and you need your credit reports if you genuinely want to look into your credit and check your background.

The first move is to clean up the records if you wish to increase your credit score. Correct any mistakes and recognize the poor places you have to strengthen (including your most extraordinary balance). However, be careful, despite the breathless email alerts that promise to lift your FIC Outlook within weeks, claiming that any improvement in your credit scores will take time.

2.5 How Credit Scores Work

Your credit score has a severe effect on your financial condition.

It has a significant impact on whether or not a lender can give you credit. Individuals with credit scores of less than 640, for example, are classified as subprime borrowers.

To cope with taking on more risk, lending institutions often charge higher interest rates on subprime mortgages than traditional mortgages. For borrowers with a low credit score, they might also need a short repayment period or a co-signer.

A 700 or higher credit score, on the other hand, is usually considered good and can entitle borrowers to a lower interest rate, resulting in them paying less money in interest and over the life of the loan.

Scores of 800 or higher are considered outstanding. Although each creditor sets its own credit score ranges, the average FICO score range is commonly used:

- Excellent is 800-850
- Very Good is 740-799
- Good is 670-739
- Fair is 580-669
- Poor is 300-579

Your credit score, which is based on a mathematical study of your creditworthiness, has a significant impact on how much you pay for any lines of credit you take out.

A person's credit score may determine the amount of an initial deposit needed to receive a mobile, cable service, or utilities and rent an apartment. And lenders look at borrowers' credit scores all the time, particularly when determining whether to change a credit card's interest rate or credit cap.

2.6 How is Your Score Calculated?

In the United States, there are three leading credit reporting agencies (Experian, Equifax, and Transunion) that monitor, update, and store consumer credit histories.

Although the data gathered by these credit bureaus can vary, there are five major factors considered when determining a credit score:

- Payment history

- Total amount owed

- Length of credit history

- Types of credit

- New credit

Payment history is 35 percent of a credit score and indicates whether or not a person pays his/her dues timely. The total amount in debt accounts for 30% of the total amount owed. It includes the credit usage percentage, which is the percentage of credit available to an individual actually used. Credit history length accounts for 15% of the score, with long credit histories is deemed less risky as more data is used to assess payment history.

The form of credit used accounts for 10percent of a credit score and indicates if an individual has a combination of installment and revolving credit, like car loans or mortgage loans.

New credit is worth 10% of a person's credit score, and it takes into account how many new accounts they have, how often new accounts have been applied for lately, which result in credit requests, and when the latest account was opened.

If you have various credit cards and want to close those linked to closing accounts that are not in your use, this will lower your ranking.

Gather the cards which you don't use instead of closing them. Keep them in separate, labeled envelopes in a safe location. To check and access each of your cards, go online.

Check for any balances and double-check that your email address, address, and other contact information are correct. Also, double-check that none of them are set to autopay.

Make sure you enter your email id or phone number in the section where you can receive alerts. Since you won't be using them, make it a point to check for fraudulent activity on them regularly.

Make a note to check them all twice a year or per year to ensure that there have been no charges and that nothing unusual has occurred.

2.7 What Is Credit Scoring? - About Types, Model and Method

A comprehensive creditworthiness review must be performed before a bank can issue a loan to a customer.

Credit scoring method

One of the most critical aspects of credit risk management is determining the degree of consumer reliability in terms of timely loan repayment. This is achieved based on the customer's attributes and a credit history review and scoring. Credit bureaus also provide information about how a customer has repaid and seeks to repay their debts. However, credit score models are used in consumer evaluation.

Credit rating is one of the tools for determining the risk linked with issuing a loan or the likelihood of non-repayment.

It is based on the customer score being calculated based on the information given in the loan application or collected from other sources. The higher a borrower's profile resembles that of those who repay their loans on time, the better their ranking.

Credit scoring is generally expressed in points, and the amount of points allows the consumer to be assigned to the acceptable risk category. Credit scoring removes the human element and guarantees objectivity in the process, lowering risk and speeding up the credit process, regardless of how it is measured or what attributes it considers.

The use of scoring models in credit processes is becoming increasingly common as a result of their various advantages:

- Server processing times are faster, resulting in lower costs.
- Goal credit risk assessment

- Increased productivity of employees

- Probability of using suitable financial collateral

- Keeping an eye on the loan portfolio for poor debts

- More accurate forecasting and credit policies

When deciding to grant a loan, several considerations are considered. This includes the borrower's characteristics, their financial status, the size of the loan requested, the loan's intent (what it would be used for), and the form of collateral.

Because of these may variables, the risk is calculated using both quantitative and qualitative methods.

The quantitative analysis begins with evaluating the customer's financial situation based on their monthly revenue and expenditures.

It can also provide a cash flow study of the customer's accounts and a review of the customer's credit history.

While the qualitative evaluation considers factors such as education, or employment status - for natural persons - and legal type, sector in which they work, or accounting method - for businesses.

Past consumer habits that have a negative impact on credit scores are also important:

- Failure to pay installments and other obligations on time

- Going over your credit card capacity

- A significant number of commitments were made.

- There is no credit history at all.

2.8 Model for Credit Scoring

Banks typically make loans based on a credit score model that incorporates both qualitative and quantitative data. Credit scoring is based on mathematical methods that allow for the prediction of the likelihood of a specific occurrence - in this case, a loan default - occurring in the future.

The scoring process uses data about the customer gathered during the application stage - primarily data about their characteristics and details about their previous actions.

Each credit institution weighs in on a specific set of factors and assigns them different point values.

A college graduate, for example, would typically score higher than a high school dropout, although the exact point value and effect on the final score will differ from bank to bank.

The final score is usually the total of points from various characteristics.

Each bank/institution determines the range of possible scores: the most common credit scoring in the United States (FICO) produces scores between 300 and 850. In contrast, the Polish credit information bureau's (BIK) scoring can reach a maximum of 100 points.

Different parameters may be used to classify scoring models. Thus, we can discuss individual or company scoring (division dependent on the assessed entity), as well as a credit card, cash, or mortgage scoring. We may speak about internal scoring or external scoring depending on who developed and handled the scoring model (created and made available by specialized institutions, e.g., credit information offices).

The distinction between implementation and behavioral scoring is very simple. The first is intended to assess new customers based on their credit application information. Behavioral ranking, on the contrary, is based on the history of a customer's behavior when it comes to financial product service. As a result, it's calculated for repeat buyers, mostly to resell new goods or adjust the terms and conditions of existing ones.

The scoring models' primary goal is to determine the likelihood of debt default. However, in recent years, there has been a growing focus on using this approach for other purposes:

- Enhancing the efficacy of marketing strategies by determining whether a consumer is likely to be interested in a particular product.

- Fraud detection,

- A scoring system for turnover,

- Enhancing debt management by deciding if the customer would be able to pay it back if financial difficulties arise.

- Maximizing profits (what credit terms should be offered to the customer to be accepted, i.e., risk-based pricing)

Regardless of the sort, scoring models allow objective credit risk assessment, an essential part of the credit-granting process. Banks are increasingly automating credit calculation and using ready-made systems that allow for a credit evaluation model in a point system to make it as reliable, straightforward, and low-risk as possible. Such methods lower the likelihood of approving dubious loans and speeds up the whole credit process, thereby lowering the chance of human error.

2.9 Individual Customer Scoring

Natural persons are assessed for risk based on individual characteristics. Education, number of dependents, type of work, seniority, occupation, and so on are the most common. Financial characteristics, such as monthly income, potential additional income, or information about expenditures, are also quite significant.

Details on the customer's financial history, such as the number of past commitments made and the background of their redemption, or information about future overdrafts, are taken into account if possible.

The list of characteristics to be included in the risk assessment varies depending on the form of credit requested. A mortgage loan's scoring model is typically more robust than a credit card's.

When purchasing a home with a loan, the scoring system considers various factors, including the property itself. It also places a greater focus on income data.

2.10 Enterprise Scoring (SME)

The risk of bankruptcy and insolvency is assessed in small and medium-sized businesses by awarding points. Their money, debt, and growth plan are all considered.

In businesses, credit is calculated based on the following factors: the industry's characteristics, the company's characteristics, and its previous financial performance.

Credit risk analysis is often conducted, with consideration given to the company's structure, source of funding, competition, and even the credentials of employees, particularly those at the highest levels.

In the case of a company, the credit evaluation model considers the company's financial state, planned ventures, liquidity, financial liabilities, and industry risk assessment.

Small
Medium
Enterprise

However, in the smallest companies, the owner of the examined company is frequently also the owner to fully assess the parameters that characterize the company. It turns out that the owner's personal credit history and profile are more important than the numbers that describe their business. This is very common in small companies that have only been on the market for a short time.

Chapter 3.
Techniques to Boost Your Credit Score

A credit score is a statistic that lenders use to determine how likely they will be regularly refunded if they give someone a loan or a credit card. Your credit history determines your credit score.

The range of your FICO Score is 300 to 850.

A good credit score is crucial for your financial security because the higher your credit score is, the little is the credit risk you have.

Generic credit scores and custom credit scores are the two most common types of credit scores:

Many forms of lenders and companies use generic credit scores to assess general credit risk. Across all three credit reporting agencies, you can view your generic score as a single score calculated using the same formula.

Person lenders create custom credit scores for them to use. They depend on credit reports and other information from the lender's portfolio, like account history. They are either exclusive to the company or are only used by such lenders, including credit unions. Various forms of loans, such as mortgages and car loans, are subjected to custom credit ratings.

3.1 Understanding Credit Score Factors

Credit score factors are the elements of your credit report that influence your credit score. Few factors that can affect credit scores are:

- Your total debt
- Types of accounts
- Number of late payments
- Age of accounts

Factors showing your credit background's aspects had the most significant impact on your credit score when it was determined.

They also tell you what problems in your credit history you need to fix to boost your creditworthiness over time.

Regularly monitoring your credit will help you keep track of how these variables influence your score and what you may be trying to do to boost it.

3.2 Why Lenders Use Credit Scores?

Until credit ratings, lenders reviewed each applicant's credit report physically to decide whether or not to extend credit.

This time-consuming procedure resulted in errors or skewed outcomes, allowing lenders to make judgments that could or may not have been based on the applicant's capacity to pay back debt. Credit scores now assist lenders in making more accurate risk assessments.

Credit ratings are objective and consistent. They only take into account your past credit history and current credit situation to determine your probability of repaying debt responsibly.

A credit score of 700 or higher is usually considered strong for a score ranging from 300 to 850.

On the same scale, a score of 800 or higher is considered outstanding.

The majority of customers have credit scores ranging from 600 to 750. The average FICO Score in the United States in 2020 was 710, up 7 points from the past year.

Creditors will be more secure in your ability to repay potential debts if your score is higher. When assessing consumers for credit cards and loans, creditors can set their own standards for what they deem to be positive or negative credit scores.

This is partly determined by the kinds of borrowers they wish to attract. Creditors can also consider how current events can influence a customer's credit score and change their criteria accordingly. Some lenders build their own custom credit scoring systems, but the FICOand VantageScore credit scoring models are the most widely used.

3.3 What Is A Good FICO Score?

FICO generates a variety of credit scores for consumers.

The company creates "base" FICO Scores for lenders in various sectors, as well as industry-specific credit scores for credit card issuers and auto lenders.FICO Scores can range from 300 to 850, with 670 to 739 being considered "healthy" by FICO.

FICOindustry-specific credit scores range from 250 to 900 points. On the other hand, the middle groups have the same groupings, and a "healthy" industry-specific FICO Score ranges from 670 to 739.

3.4 What Is A Good Vantagescore?

The first two VantageScore credit scoring models range from 501 to 990. The 300 to 850 range is used for the two latest VantageScore credit scores (3.0 and 4.0), which are the same as base FICO Scores. VantageScore finds 661 to 780 to be a decent range for the most recent models.

3.5 What Affects Your Credit Scores?

All of your credit scores are affected by common factors, which are usually divided into five categories:

- Payment history: Making on-time payments with your credit cards will help you improve your credit scores. However, failing to make payments, getting an account sent to collections, or declaring bankruptcy may all lower your credit scores.

- Credit usage: This factor considers how much balance is there on your accounts, how much you owe, and how much of your credit limits you're using on revolving accounts.

- Credit history length: This category contains the total age of all of your credit accounts, as well as the oldest and newest accounts.

- Account types: Also known as "credit mix," this element considers whether you're handling both installment and revolving accounts (such as a car loan, personal loan, or mortgage). Demonstrating that you can responsibly handle all forms of accounts increases your overall ranking.

- Recent activity: This factor considers whether you've requested or opened a new account in the last few months.

The relative value of the groups is explained differently by FICOand VantageScore.

3.6 Factors That Affect Your FICO Score

Although the exact %age breakdown used to calculate your credit score will depend on your particular credit report, FICOuses percentages to reflect how relevant each category is in general. The following is the order in which FICOconsiders scoring factors:

- Payment history: 35%

- Length of credit history: 15%

- Amounts owed: 30%

- New credit: 10%

- Credit mix: 10%

3.7 Factors That Affect Your Vantagescore

VantageScore rates the variables in order of how relevant they are in calculating a credit score, although this can differ depending on your credit report.

The following considerations are taken into account by VantageScore:

• Credit utilization, balance, and available credit: All have a significant impact.

• Credit utilization, balance, and available credit: All have a significant impact.

3.8 What Information Credit Scores Do Not Consider?

When calculating credit scores, FICO and VantageScore do not take into account the following information:

- Your ethnicity, nationality, national origin, gender, or marital status. (These facts, and any receipt of social aid or the practice of any consumer right under the Consumer Credit Protection Act, are not taken into account by credit rating formulas in the United States.)

- Your age

- Your wage, job description, employer, date of employment, or work history. (However, keep in mind that lenders can take this information into account when making overall approval decisions.)

- Your residence.

- Investigations that are not aggressive. Others, such as companies making promotional credit offers or your lender undertaking periodic reviews of your current credit accounts, usually initiate soft inquiries. When you search your credit report or use credit monitoring services from organizations such as Experian, soft inquiries occur as well. Your credit ratings are unaffected by these inquiries.

3.9 Why Are There Different Credit Scores?

Lenders use credit scores as a metric when making lending decisions. FICO and VantageScore both create credit scoring models for lenders. Both companies release new versions of their credit scoring models regularly, similar to how other software companies release new operating systems. The most recent versions may incorporate technological advancements or changes in consumer behavior and meet new regulatory requirements.

VantageScore, for example, uses a tri-bureau scoring model, which means it can assess your credit report from any of the three leading consumer credit bureaus (TransUnion, Experian, and Equifax).

In 2006, the first version, VantageScore 1.0, was released. VantageScore 4.0, the most recent version, was released in 2017 and was based on data from 2014 to 2016.

The first generic credit score included trended data or information about how people manage their accounts over time.

FICO is a more established company that was among the first to develop credit scoring models due to consumer credit reports. It creates various versions of its scoring models for each credit bureau's data, though recent versions, such as FICO Score 8, have a common name. There are two widely used kinds of consumer FICO Scores:

- Base FICO Scores: These scores are designed to predict the likelihood of a consumer defaulting on any type of credit obligation, and any lender can use them. FICO credit scores start at 300 and go up to 850.

- FICO Scores for Auto Lenders and Bankcard Issuers: FICO produces auto and bankcard scores exclusively for auto lenders and card issuers. Industry scores can vary from 250 to 900 and estimate the probability of a customer defaulting on a particular form of account.

FICO industry-specific scores are developed on top of a base FICO Score, and new suites of scores are released regularly.

For example, the FICO Score Ten Suite was announced earlier in 2020. It includes a FICO Score 10 base score, a FICO Score 10 T (with trended data), and new industry-specific scores.

—

Scores are often used on a more infrequent basis.

FICO, for example, is gradually introducing the UltraFICO Score, which enables customers to connect checking, savings, and money market accounts and takes banking activity into account.

Lenders may also build personalized credit score models that are tailored to their specific customers.

Lenders can use whatever model they want. Many lenders may opt to stick with earlier versions due to the potential investment needed to move.

Many mortgage lenders still use previous versions of the base FICO Scores to meet with government-sponsored mortgage companies Fannie Mae and Freddie Mac's guidelines.

You won't always know which score and credit report a lender would use until after you've applied.

The good news is that both consumer VantageScore and FICOcredit scores are based on the same underlying data—information from one of your credit reports.

They all strive to make the same prediction: the probability that a person will be Ninety days past due on a bill (of any type) over the next 24 months.

As a consequence, the credit scores can be affected by the same factors.

If you monitor several credit scores, you can notice that your results vary based on the scoring model and which of your credit reports it examines.

However, you will find that they all appear to change over time together.

3.10 Why Having a Good Credit Score Is Important?

Usually, good credit will facilitate the achievement of your personal and financial objectives. There may be a difference between being approved for a large loan or being rejected for a home loan or car loan. And if you are allowed, it will affect directly how much you pay for interest or charges.

For instance, there may be $72 a month to distinguish between a 30-year $250,000 fixed mortgage with a FICO Score of 670 and a FICO Score of 720. You may put additional money towards your investments or other financial objectives. Without a decent ranking, you can save $26,071 in interest payments over your lifetime.

Credit rates can also affect non-lending decisions, for example, when a landlord agrees to rent an apartment to you.

You may also influence the credit reports. Before deciding to hire or promote, some employers can check your credit reports. And insurance companies can, in most countries, use credit-based insurance ratings to help calculate car, home, and life insurance premiums.

Chapter 4.

Smart Strategies to Build Good Credit

It is possible to live with poor credit, but it is not always simple or inexpensive. A decent credit score will allow you to save money and simplify your financial life.

If you're trying to find a reason to keep your good credit, consider the following advantages of getting a good credit score.

4.1 Low-Interest Rates on Credit Cards and Loans

The interest rate is among the costs associated with borrowing money, and it is also directly related to your credit score. You'll also often qualify for the most excellent interest rates and pay lower finance costs on credit card balances and loans if you have a decent credit score. The less interest you pay, the sooner you'll be able to pay off your debt and have more money for other things.

4.2 Better Chance for Credit Card and Loan Approval

Borrowers with a bad credit history are also hesitant to apply for a new loan from a bank because they have already been denied.

Since lenders consider other variables such as your income and debt, having a good credit score isn't guaranteed approval.

A strong credit score, on the other hand, increases the chances of getting new credit. In other terms, you can confidently apply for a loan or a credit card.

4.3 More Negotiating Power

With a decent credit score, you will get a better interest rate on a credit card or a new loan. If you need more negotiating leverage, you can use other appealing deals depending on your credit score that you've earned from other businesses.

Creditors are reluctant to back down on loan terms if you have a poor credit score, and you won't have any other credit deals or options.

4.4 Get Approved for Higher Limits

Your income and credit score determine your borrowing power.

One of the advantages of getting a strong credit score is that banks are more likely to let you take out loans because you've shown that you repay your debts on time. With a bad credit score, you might still be eligible for some loans, but the amount will be limited.

4.5 Easier Approval for Rental Houses and Apartments

Landlords are increasingly using credit scores as one of their tenant selection processes.

A poor credit score, mainly if it's the result of a prior eviction or an unpaid rental balance, may make it difficult to find an apartment.

A decent credit score saves you the effort and time of searching for a landlord who would rent to people with bad credit.

4.6 Better Car Insurance Rates

Auto insurers are among the firms that would use a low credit score against you. Insurance companies build your insurance risk score using statistics from your credit report and insurance background, so people with poor credit scores also face higher insurance premiums.

You'll pay less for insurance if you have a decent credit score than if you have a bad credit score.

4.7 Get a Cell Phone on Contract with No Security Deposit

Another disadvantage of getting a low credit score is that cell phone companies can refuse to give you a contract.

Instead, you'll have to pick from one of the more costly pay-as-you-go plans. You may have to pay more money on your contract before you've formed a relationship with the provider, at the very least. By signing a contract, people with good credit will avoid paying a security deposit and get a discount on the new phones.

4.8 Avoid Security Deposits on Utilities

These deposits can range from $100 to $200, and they're a pain to deal with while you're moving.

You may not have been planning to relocate anytime soon, but a major catastrophe or unexpected circumstances may cause you to reconsider. When you set up a utility service under your name or switch service to another venue, you won't be paying a security deposit if you have a good credit score.

4.9 Bragging Rights

A good credit score is something to be proud of because of all the benefits, mainly if you've worked hard to improve your credit score from bad to good. And if you've never had a poor credit score before, keep doing what you can to keep it that way. It just takes a few unpaid bills to fall behind on your payments.

When information on a borrower's credit report is updated, their credit score change, and new information can cause their credit score to rise or fall. Here are some suggestions for improving a consumer's credit score:

Pay your bills on time: It takes six months of on-time payments to see a significant difference in your credit score.

Increase your credit limit: If you have credit cards, call and ask for a credit limit increase. If your account is in top form, you should be given a credit limit increase. It's critical not to splurge this amount to keep your credit utilization rate low.

Don't close a credit card account: It's better to stop using a credit card than to close the account if you're not using it. Closing a credit card account can harm your credit score, depending on its age and credit limit. Assume you owe $1,000 and have a $5,000 credit limit divided equally between two credit cards. Your credit utilization rate is currently 20%, which is acceptable. Closing one of the cards, on the other hand, would increase your credit utilization rate to 40%, which would have a negative effect on your credit score.

Hire one of the top credit repair companies: If you don't have time to work on your credit, credit repair companies will start negotiating with your creditors and the three credit bureaus on your behalf for a monthly fee. Furthermore, given the variety of opportunities that a good credit score opens up, it may be worthwhile to use one of the most important credit monitoring services to keep your data safe.

4.10 Ways to Improve Your Credit Scores

Depend on the fundamental factors that influence your credit scores to increase your credit scores.

The basic steps that must be taken are pretty simple at a high level:

- Make at least the minimum contribution and for-time payments on all of your debts. A single late payment will harm your credit ratings, and it can remain on your credit report for up to 7 years. If you think you'll miss a bill, contact your creditors right away to see if they can negotiate with you or have hardship solutions.

- Maintain a low credit card balance. The credit limit and current balance of revolving accounts like credit cards are compared in your credit utilization rate, which is a significant scoring factor. Your credit score can be boosted by providing a low credit utilization rate. The average usage rate of those with outstanding credit scores is usually in the single figures.

- Accounts with open balances that will be submitted to credit bureaus. If you have a limited number of credit accounts, ensure that any new ones you open are added to your credit report. Installment accounts, like student, vehicle, home, or personal loans, as well as revolving accounts, like credit cards and lines of credit, are examples.

- Apply for credit only when you really need it. Applying for a new account will result in a hard investigation, which will negatively impact your credit scores. Although the effect is typically small, applying for a large number of different forms of loans or credit cards in a short time will result in a larger score decrease.

Your scores can be affected by several other variables. Having a higher age of your accounts, for example, could improve your scores. However, waiting rather than acting is often the case.

Having checked your credit scores will also help you figure out what you can do to boost them.

When you review your free FICO Score 8 from Experian, you can see how you're doing in every one of the credit score categories, for example.

4.11 What to Do if You Don't Have a Credit Score?

Credit scoring models utilize your credit reports to measure your ranking, but they can't score reports with insufficient data.

To get your FICO Scores, you'll need:

- A six-month-old account
- An account active for at least the last six months

Even if the account is just a month old, VantageScore will rate your credit report if it has at least a single account.

To start building credibility, you can have to open a new account or add additional activity to your credit report if you aren't scoreable.

Beginning with a credit-builder loan with a secured credit card, or being an approved customer, is always the best way to go.

4.12 Why Does Your Credit Score Change?

Your credit score will change for various reasons, and when new information is applied to your credit reports, it's not unusual for scores to fluctuate during the month.

You may also be able to identify a particular occurrence that triggers a difference in your ranking. A late payment or a new collection account, for example, would almost lower your credit score.

Paying down a large credit card balance and lowering your utilization rate, on the other hand, can improve your credit score.

However, certain acts can have unanticipated repercussions for your credit scores.

Paying off a loan, for instance, can result in a decrease in your credit score, even though it is a good thing in terms of effective money management.

This may be because your only open installment account and maybe the only loan with a lower balance on your credit report. After paying off the loan, you can be left with only high-balance loans or a combination of open installments and revolving accounts.

After paying off your credit card balances, you might simply stop using them. Although it is a good idea to avoid debt, your accounts' lack of activity can result in a lower credit score.

To keep your account active and create an on-time payment history, you may need to use a card for a limited monthly subscription and afterward pay off the balance in full every month.

Remember that credit scoring models rely on complex equations to arrive at a final score.

You might believe that one occurrence caused your score to rise or fall, but it was just a coincidence.

Also, a single incident isn't "worth" a certain number of points; the entire credit report determines points you gain or lose.

A new late payment, for example, may result in a significant point decrease for someone who has never been late beforehand, as it could signify a change in conduct and, as a result, an increase in credit risk.

Someone who has previously missed many payments, on the other hand, will see a smaller point decrease from a recent late payment since it is expected that they will continue to miss payments.

4.13 Checking Your Credit Score

It used to be challenging to check your credit score. Today, however, there are many choices for checking your credit scores, such as several free options.

One of your credit scores may be available for free from your credit union, bank, lender, or credit card issuer. You can get a free FICO Score depending on your credit report from Experian.

Depending on the source, you will earn a different credit score. Some services can provide you with a FICO Score replica, while others provide VantageScore credit scores.

In any case, the measured score is influenced by the credit report that the scoring model examines.

You can also review several credit scores at once for specific providers.

For example, you could get your FICO Score Eight scores depending on your Experian, Equifax, and TransUnion credit reports, as well as several other FICO Scores dependent on your Experian credit report, with an Experian CreditWorksSM Premium membership.

Testing your credit score just before applying for a new loan or credit card will help you to understand your chances of getting favorable terms. But checking it much more ahead of time will help you boost your score and potentially save lots of money in interest. Experian provides free credit monitoring on your Experian report, which contains warnings about a questionable change in your report concerning a free score and report.

Keeping track of your credit score will help you take steps to boost it, increasing your chances of getting a loan, credit card, apartment, or insurance policy while also enhancing your financial health.

Chapter 5.

Fixing Bad Credit

A good credit score can aid in purchasing a home, the startup of a company, or the acquisition of a car loan.

A decent credit score makes life easier. This three-digit number influences virtually every aspect of your financial life. It makes significant milestones such as renting an apartment, purchasing a car, or obtaining a mortgage on your first home more manageable.

5.1 Why do You Need a Good Credit Score?

Learn how to get on the road to stellar credit, whether you're a recent high school graduate or building credit later in life. Why is it essential to have a good credit score?

Getting a good credit score isn't difficult, but it's crucial for your overall financial situation. You'll have a better time being accepted for an apartment if you've got a decent or outstanding credit score, you'll get better deals on car and homeowner's insurance, and borrowing money when you need it will be less expensive.

When faced with an unforeseen financial crisis, such as a layoff, having a good credit score can be particularly beneficial. If lenders see you as a reliable borrower, you'll be more likely to get favorable deals for 0% financing if you ever need it.

A decent credit score also grants you access to great rewards credit cards, including cash back, travel benefits, purchase insurance, and luxury benefits.

Fortunately, once you understand how credit works, it's not difficult to build a good credit score. This guide will take you through the basics step-by-step, so you can fully comprehend how your credit score is measured, how to build good credit, and how to keep it in the longer term.

5.2 What is a Good Credit Score?

Credit scores range from 300 to 850, with 300 indicating mediocre credit and 850 indicating excellent credit. Credit score levels differ depending on the credit scoring model utilized (FICO vs. VantageScore) and the pulling score credit bureau (Equifax, Experian, and TransUnion). The credit ranges for the two most common scoring models are listed below:

FICO Score Credit Ranges

- Very poor: 300 to 579

- Fair: 580 to 669

- Good: 670 to 739

- Very good: 740 to 799

- Excellent: 800 to 850

VantageScore credit ranges

- Very poor: 300 to 499

- Poor: 500 to 600

- Fair: 601 to 660

- Good: 661 to 780

- Excellent: 781 to 850

If your lender uses Experian to obtain your credit score, they can see your FICO credit score. To have a decent credit score, you'll need a score between 670 and 739.

Sadly, there really is no way to know which credit score model will be used by your lender. Lenders ask one of the three credit bureaus for your records, and they don't all use the same one.

5.3 The Difference Between Excellent and Good Credit Score

The best credit score you can get is "Excellent." It ranges from 800 to 850 on the FICO scale and from 781 to 850 on the VantageScore scale. It's challenging to achieve a perfect credit score of 850, but an outstanding credit score is more attainable.

Many of the best credit cards necessitate excellent or decent credit. You'll need a decent credit score to take advantage of lucrative incentives, annual statement credits, luxurious travel benefits, 0% APR periods, and more. You will also increase your chances of acceptance if you've got a decent credit score.

For example, suppose you want to receive generous discounts on food and eating out. In that case, the American Express Gold Card gives you 4X Membership Rewards points when you eat dinner at restaurants around the world and shop at U.S. supermarkets (on transactions up to $25,000 a year, then 1X). However, to be eligible for Amex Gold, which CNBC Select called the 2020 best rewards card, you'll need decent or excellent credit.

You'll also need decent or excellent credit to fund new purchases or pay off debt with a balance transfer card like the Chase Freedom Unlimited.

Even if your credit score is outstanding, it does not mean you would be accepted for a credit card that needs excellent credit. Card issuers consider various variables in addition to your credit scores, such as your salary and monthly housing payments.

5.4 The Drawbacks of Getting A Bad or Fair Credit Rating

A poor or fair credit score may significantly affect your overall financial situation, affecting the types of loans and goods you are eligible for.

A poor score ranges from 300 to 579 on the FICO scoring model, while a fair score ranges from 580 to 669.

A very poor credit score ranges from 300 to 499 points, a poor credit score ranges from 500 to 600 points, and a decent credit score ranges from 601 to 660 points.

The following are three drawbacks to getting a poor or fair credit score:

- You'll have a harder time getting credit cards or loans.

- If you are accepted, the loan terms would be less favorable.

- Your credit card options will be restricted.

Credit cards and loans are less likely to be accepted.

A low credit score can make it difficult to obtain credit cards and loans, making certain goals difficult to achieve. You'll need decent or excellent credit to use a balance transfer card to get out of debt. It would be almost impossible to find a card that allows poor credit if you want to collect rewards or enjoy luxurious travel benefits.

If you are accepted, the loan terms would be less favorable.

Compared to applicants with good credit, you're more likely to be given less desirable terms, including high interest rates or annual fees, if you're accepted for credit. The OpenSky Protected Visa Credit Card, for example, is one of CNBC Select's best credit cards for poor credit, with a $35 annual fee; however, there are no annual fee choices.

5.5 The Most Significant Disadvantages of a Bad Credit Score

The majority of customers in the United States currently have a decent credit score or better, but reaching there can be challenging. The eight main obstacles of getting a bad credit score and how to break the loop are covered in CNBC Select.

You will get premium credit cards, better loan options, and lower interest rates if you have a decent credit score.

If you've got a low credit score — say, 300 to 579 on the FICO scale or 300 to 600 on the VantageScore scale — you'll miss out on these offers and end up paying even more in interest on credit cards, loans, and mortgages.

A poor credit score can make things challenging in various ways, including delaying retirement and costing you more money in the long run. However, raising your credit score takes more than chance, and it's only achievable if you realize how important your credit score is to your life.

5.6 Breaking the Bad Credit Cycle

Here are the outlines, the first step you can take to break the cycle of bad credit.

1. You're too risky for primary lenders.

When you have a bad credit score, you will not be eligible for conventional loans or credit cards because banks have stringent criteria for deciding who qualifies for lending.

"The effect of a poor credit score is that the mainstream funding access is nonexistent or limited."

However, Ulzheimer recommends that you read the fine print before taking out a loan from a less-than-reputable source such as a payday loan, pawnshop, or title loan business.

Payday loans, for instance, are a convenient way to get quick cash when you need it, but they come with warnings indicating that the annual percentage rate (APR) will range from 400 percent to 700 percent. According to Ulzheimer, these must be avoided at all costs.

2. You pay more for your loan

A decent credit score will not only help you with more trustworthy banks, but it will also get you the best loan interest rates. According to Ulzheimer, customers who have a credit score of 720 or higher on car loans and 750 or higher on mortgages get the best APR rates. Assume you have a FICO score of 620 and are applying for a mortgage. With today's rates, a $300,000 house would cost about 4.8 percent in interest, while a buyer with a credit score of 760 to 850 would pay about 3.2 percent APR.

A 1.6 percent difference may seem insignificant, but in this situation, your lower credit score will raise your monthly mortgage payment by around $275, costing you $99,000 over the course of 30 years.

3. Your insurance premiums may go up

Most states in the United States enable credit-based insurance scoring, allowing auto and homeowners insurance firms to consider your financial activities when determining your risk.

If your credit score falls below 600, your premium will not automatically increase, nor will your policy be canceled.

However, if you have a poor credit score, you might not get the best deal. You will get a report from LexisNexis if you want to examine your credit-based insurance ranking.

(Note: In Hawaii, credit-based auto insurance scoring is prohibited, while in Maryland, credit-based home insurance scoring is prohibited.) Massachusetts and California have outright outlawed the practice.)

4. You may miss out on career opportunities

You'll have more work prospects if you have good credit habits. Employers are required to pull consumer credit reports in most states when making hiring decisions and determine who to hire or reassign.

This is especially true if the work requires a great deal of financial responsibility.

Your employer will not see your exact credit score. Still, if you give them signed permission, they will have access to your credit report.

They will be able to see details such as open lines of credit, any delinquent balances, car loans, past foreclosures, student loans, late or missed payments, bankruptcies, and collections balances.

5. You will have a tough time renting the apartment

According to Experian, a 620 credit score is often the bare minimum needed to apply for an apartment.

Some property management firms and landlords are more strict than others, so you should rest easy if your credit score is 700 or higher. If your reputation is bad, you can need to find a co-signer or pay a security deposit before signing a new lease. Renting an apartment with bad credit isn't impossible, but it can be a lot more complicated.

6. You will have a more challenging time with utilities, which also includes the internet

"Utility companies can charge deposits when you've got a credit score bad," Ulzheimer says. "And I do not know the utility companies that are going to give you an account without a background check."

There are provisions in some states against losing access to public services such as water, electricity, gas, and heat.

Suppose you have bad credit and are refused access to energy utilities.

In that case, you will be able to pay a deposit or apply a letter of guarantee, which serves as a guarantor or co-signer agreement if you fall behind on your bills.

There are fewer legal safeguards in non-public infrastructures such as cable and internet to ensure access to these facilities. However, the United Nations already considers internet access to be a human right.

7. You won't enjoy the best rewards credit cards

The highest credit scores are required for the best rewards credit cards.

When your credit score is decent or outstanding, you can take advantage of the best introductory deals and cashback bonuses currently available in the credit market.

Some high-tier credit cards provide exclusive access to pre-sale tickets to concerts and events, as well as cashback on streaming services.

The Capital One Savor Cash Rewards Credit Card is one of CNBC Select's top picks for cashback cards, whether you're a sports fan, a movie buff, or an adventure seeker.

It provides a competitive cashback rate of 4% on food and entertainment, 2% on groceries, and 1% on all other transactions.

After spending $3,000 on transactions within the first three months of account opening, new cardholders will receive a one-time $300 cash bonus.

8. You delay building wealth — and even retiring

Bad credit may have a long-term financial effect on your life. You won't be able to save much money for the future if you have high-interest credit card debt, at least not enough to cover your APR fees.

You're putting less money into investment and assets and more money into debt servicing as long as the interest rates are high. And debt has no payback; the money you pay in interest is money you'll never see again.

In some cases, eligible customers should seek a balance transfer credit card like the Aspire Platinum Mastercard, which offers a 0% APR for a limited time. If you have a current debt to pay off, a balance transfer card will help you save money on interest payments.

Your credit score could increase when you decrease your debt-to-credit ratio, and it may be worth repaying your mortgage or car loans to see if you can get a better APR, shave some interest off, and set it away for retirement savings.

5.7 Breaking the Loop of Poor Credit

"If you've poor credit, you know it probably," Ulzheimer says. You might feel embarrassed, worried, or guilty, but you are likely "not going to be astonished if you pulled the credit and found delinquent & defaulted accounts."

The most significant explanation why people with terrible credit scores don't change them is because they're stuck in a loop.

Think this way, Ulzheimer says: "You can throw out the pizza if you screw it and pop another in the oven. But credit is a self-policing and very punishing environment."

To put it another way, it's not easy to start over. Delinquencies (accounts that are past due for more than 30 days) are reported on your credit report for at least seven years.

However, Ulzheimer advises customers that seven years is not a life sentence unless they try to "restart the clock" by skipping payments.

5.8 Options for Getting Out of Debt

According to Ulzheimer, the first step to breaking free from the debt cycle is to "press the reset button."

Talking with a nonprofit credit counselor, partnering with a debt advisor, filing for bankruptcy, or even remaining out of the credit game for a few years if necessary are all options.

"You might need to take a break for a while," Ulzheimer says, suggesting that you put your credit cards away.

If you should apply for one of CNBC Select's best credit cards for poor credit, he warns that you should expect "punitive words."

An annual fee (with no incentives to compensate), a higher-than-average APR, or even a secured credit card, such as the Discover it Secured Credit Card, which includes a $200 security deposit, are all possibilities.

It is possible to increase your credit score if you have a bad credit score. The poor marks can be removed for delinquencies after seven years, and for bankruptcy, after ten years.

If you avoid taking on more debt and pay your bills on time, your credit score will gradually improve. Paying the minimum payment each month would, at the very least, help you boost your payment history and lower your debt-to-credit ratio.

Meanwhile, you should read about the most popular credit card blunders, so you can feel comfortable using one again and know how to adhere to your terms and agreements.

Ulzheimer says, "Many people fall into the pit of thinking that if they pay almost enough to meet the minimum bill, even if they miss the due date by just a few days, it should still count, and they should not be penalized,"

"However, if you can break away from this way of thinking, you can wake up someday with a higher ranking. I guarantee you that you are no more than seven years away from excellent credit."

To make transactions and make financial choices, society has become increasingly reliant on credit.

A decent credit score will help you get more than a credit card or a loan. Credit ratings show how well you've paid off debts owed to financial institutions.

Many citizens are unable to settle their debts because they have gone beyond their means. Around the same time, people's paychecks are being depleted by general living expenses. Companies have reasonable reason to demand that you have good credit before offering goods or services on credit.

Some employers are also conducting credit checks to determine whether or not you can be entrusted with company funds or assets. You may have trouble finding jobs if you have a record of not being financially responsible.

Credit Can Affect Where You Live

Mortgage lenders want to assume that you won't default on your loan before you can buy a home. If you don't have good credit, a lender would think it's risky to lend you money.

Your credit influences your interest rate if you're accepted for a mortgage. Interest rates directly affect your monthly mortgage payment, rising or reducing the amount you pay.

A loan application with a poor credit score would be rejected or accepted at a higher rate. Even if you aren't looking for a home right now, your credit is still valuable. Landlords look at your credit score when determining whether or not to rent to you.

Rental property is treated as a loan, and owners want to know that they will be paid.

Good credit is required for auto loans

The majority of people do not have enough money to both fund a car and cover their living expenses. Many people would apply for a car loan.

Your credit score affects whether you are eligible, the money you can borrow, and the loan's interest rate. Loan borrowers with a higher credit score typically qualify for greater loan amounts and lower interest rates.

Your options will be limited if you have a poor credit rating. If you have bad credit, few lenders will deal with you, and those who do will give you a much higher interest rate on your car loan. A higher interest rate will increase the monthly amount you pay on the vehicle, which will increase the overall amount you pay over time.

Credit Checks For Employment

As part of the recruiting process, several companies run credit checks. (It's worth noting that employers look at credit reports rather than credit scores.) Credit reports are not permitted to be used by prospective employers in some states.)

A prospective employer may be reluctant to recruit you if you haven't demonstrated financial responsibility.

For instance, the employer may believe that your debt load is too high for the provided salary.

Some employers review credit reports before giving a promotion or increase, particularly for financially related or executive positions.

Business Loans Require Good Credit

Many people fantasize about starting their own business. Most company startups necessitate a substantial sum of money, which you may not have.

You'll need to get a small business loan in that situation. To qualify for a business loan, you must have good credit, among other items.

Expenses for living will necessitate good credit.

It can come as a surprise to know that your credit is required to set up utility services. Three electric companies say that you are borrowing one month's worth of electricity.

The company will check your credit before switching on your electricity.

Many utility systems, including cable, internet, water, and even mobile phone service providers, perform credit checks.

To live comfortably, you'll need good credit.

Many businesses—mortgage lenders, landlords, utility companies, and even employers—use your credit to assess your future financial obligation because your credit is determined by how you've paid (or not paid) your bills in the past.

Any time you need to borrow money, fund a necessary object, or set up facilities, your payment history (credit) is scrutinized.

Your credit report and credit score are almost the same, right? Far from that. Since there is a reasonable number of customers, the information used by each of the two is for a different purpose.

- A credit report is a thorough review of your finances in one venue.

- It includes comprehensive financial history data gathered in four categories: identifying information, credit inquiries, credit accounts, and public records.

- A credit score is a statistical rating that values your credit report in the similar way a teacher rates a student's educational performance.

- Lenders are used to determining whether to offer you loans as a shortcut.

5.9 How to Rebuild Your Credit File After Bankruptcy

If you're having a hard time with the financial burden, bankruptcy can be a solution. It offers you the possibility to get the help you require, as well as to work towards a debt-free life.

Bankruptcy is a way to reduce your debt when you are not able to repay them. You should consider it a last resort that you should use only when you have already exhausted all other possible methods to repair your debt.

Individuals filing for bankruptcy can use either Chapter 7 or Chapter 13. The most significant difference between is about your property:

⇒ **Chapter 7**, also known as liquidation bankruptcy, concerns selling some or all of your property to pay off your debts. This is often the choice if you have a limited income.

⇒ **Chapter 13**, which is known as reorganization bankruptcy, involves keeping your property (including your home and car) if you perform a court-mandated repayment plan that lasts three to five years.

As missed payments and high balances are the top factors influencing your credit score, your credit may not be in great shape after filing for bankruptcy.

Bankruptcy will affect your credit scores and creditworthiness the whole time it appears on your credit report. However, that impact will decrease as time passes. Chapter 7 bankruptcy stays on your report for up to 10 years, and Chapter 13 for up to seven years.

Obviously, it is not an excellent credit position, but you can use the time to control your debts and make regular on-time payments.

With focus and patience, it is possible to rebuild your credit after bankruptcy and get back on track financially.

Repairing your credit after bankruptcy can seem discouraging, but there are some actions you can take to help your credit history begin to recover:

⇒ **Pay on time in the future.** Sometimes, the bankruptcy court will enable you to keep some accounts open. If you still have open and active accounts included in the bankruptcy, be sure to make every payment on time.

⇒ **Open a new account.** If you are starting from scratch with no remaining open accounts, it can be challenging to qualify for new credit after bankruptcy. Consider opening a secured credit card, getting a credit-builder loan, or asking a friend or family member to add you as an authorized user on their credit card. Making small purchases and then paying the balance in full each month will help build a positive payment history, which can help offset the negative impact of bankruptcy.

⇒ **heck your credit report frequently.** Keep track of your credit situation by reviewing your credit report frequently. You can also request your free credit score from Experian, which will include a list of the top risk factors impacting your scores.

5.10 How to Remove Bankruptcy from Your Credit Report

According to the Chapter you file, you can delete bankruptcy from your credit report after 7 or 10 years.

A Chapter 7 bankruptcy will be cleared after ten years from the bankruptcy filing date; instead, a Chapter 13 bankruptcy will be removed after seven years.

Removing a bankruptcy from your credit report earlier than these schedules can be a complicated process, but it is possible to do if you take the following actions.

Get a copy of all three of your credit reports and check for any errors.

If you find inaccurate information, you should immediately dispute the bankruptcy record with the credit bureaus.

If the credit bureaus cannot verify the bankruptcy, they will remove it from your credit report.
This is rarely the case if bankruptcy is recent, but it could happen with an old bankruptcy.
If it happens, you have reached your goal to remove bankruptcy from your credit report earlier. However, if the credit bureaus verify the bankruptcy, you can proceed with another move.

Follow up with the credit bureau for additional verification.

You should send a procedural request letter in which you ask the credit bureaus who they verified the bankruptcy with.
The bureaus will reply and state that they verified with the courts. But here's the thing: the courts usually don't verify bankruptcies for any credit agency. You can use this to your advantage. Here's the way to do it.

You shall contact the courts and ask them how they verified the bankruptcy. They will likely say they didn't verify anything. Ask for this declaration in written form.

When you receive the court's letter, you should mail it to the credit bureaus and request that they promptly remove the bankruptcy as they deliberately provided inaccurate information and consequently are in violation of the Fair Credit Reporting Act. Accordingly, the credit bureaus will remove the bankruptcy from your report.

Even if this process is time-consuming, complicated and there is no guarantee that it will work, it's worth trying.
Of course, if you don't want to waste too much time on this method, you can outsource the entire matter to a professional credit repair company.

Chapter 6.
Section 609 Success

6.1 What is Section 609 and How Does It Work?

Section 609 is a part of the Fair Credit Reporting Act (FCRA), which specifies a customer's right to get a copy of their credit report and its information. Section 609 doesn't clearly discuss your right to dispute incorrect details. However, it states your right to a copy of all your credit file info and your right to dispute details you believe to be inaccurate or unverifiable.

Under this section, you have the right to request all of the info in your consumer credit files and the source of that info. You also have the right to request each prospective company that has accessed your credit report within the past two years and the companies that have made soft queries within the past year.

Credit reporting companies are responsible for eliminating any disputed details that can't be confirmed or validates. They're moreover bound to provide a description of the dispute process if you request it in writing. If the information is proved to be accurate, the bureaus aren't required to discharge it.

According to the credit bureaus' duty to report only validated information, you can dispute errors with a 609 letter. The theory behind the 609 letters is that asking your financial institutions to produce hard-to-find details-- such as the original signed copy of your credit application-- would make it tough to validate a contested product.

Under the rights managed to you by the FCRA, a 609 letter might assist you in getting rid of incorrect or inaccurate details in your credit report. The drawback is that if the furnisher effectively validates its precision, the info can be added back to your file.

Obviously, you're still obligated to pay back any genuine debts, even if the credit bureaus delete the info from your file.

If the info is proper and real, it may remain on your credit report. In that case, you should write again to the credit bureau and request the disclosure of details under section 609 of the Fair Credit Reporting Act.

If the dispute stands, the credit bureaus will eliminate the negative item. Any precise or verifiable info will stay on your credit report-- a 609 letter doesn't guarantee its elimination.

6.2 Dispute Letter Templates

Section 609 Letter Template #1

[Date]
[Your Name]
[Your Address]
[Your City, State, Zip Code]
[Your Account Number]

[Name of Company/Point Person]
[Relevant Department]
[Address]
[City, State, Zip Code]

Dear [Name of credit reporting agency],

I am writing to exercise my right to question the validity of the debt your agency claims I owe pursuant to the Fair Credit Reporting Act (FCRA).

As stated in Section 609 of the FCRA, (2) (E): A consumer reporting agency is not required to remove accurate derogatory information from a consumer's file unless the information is outdated under Section 609 or cannot be verified.

As is my right, I am requesting verification of the following items:

[List any/all items you're looking to dispute, including the account name(s) and number(s) as listed on your credit report]

Additionally, I have highlighted these items on the attached copy of the credit report I received.

I request that all future correspondence be done through the mail or email. As stated in the FCRA, you are required to respond to my dispute within 30 days of receipt of this letter. If you fail to offer a response, all disputed information must be deleted.

Thank you for your prompt attention to this matter.

Sincerely
[Your signature]

See Attached: [List attached documents here.]
[Attach copies of proof of identity (name, birth date, SSN, current mailing address) along with a copy of your credit report with relevant items highlighted]

Source: https://www.creditrepairexpert.org/609-letter/

Section 609 Follow up Letter Template

[Date]
[Your Name]
[Your Address]
[Your City, State, Zip Code]
[Your Account Number]

[Name of Company/Point Person]
 [Relevant Department]
[Address]
[City, State, Zip Code]

Dear Sir or Madam,

My name is [Your name], and I reached out to you several weeks ago regarding my credit report. This letter is to notify you that you have not responded to my initial letter, dated [insert date]. I have restated the terms of my dispute below for your convenience.

[Insert information from your first letter about disputed items. Include disputed account names and numbers as listed on your credit report.]

Section 609 of the Fair Credit Reporting Act (FCRA) states that you must investigate my dispute within 30 calendar days from my initial letter. As you have failed to do so, I kindly request that you remove the aforementioned items from my credit report.
Any further comments or questions can be directed to my legal representative, [insert name], who can be reached at [insert phone number].

Sincerely,

[Your signature]

See Attached: [List all attached documentation here, including copies of your credit report, proof of identity, proof of current mailing address, etc.]

Source: https://www.creditrepairexpert.org/609-letter/

CPSIA information can be obtained
at www.ICGtesting.com
Printed in the USA
BVHW090010080621
608941BV00004B/1098